Sing a Song

A book of words made for music

Jochen C. E. Hylbert

Copyright © 2019 Jahkin Publishing

All rights reserved.

ISBN:
978-1-7337506-0-8

DEDICATION

This work is dedicated to my three children:
Jordan, Julia & James

ACKNOWLEDGMENTS

I would like to thank my Mom and Dad for instilling a love of nature and humanity from a young age.

I want to thank Margot for all of the Love, positive energy and support!

I am grateful for the life-long friendships of the "On Wisconsin" crew and our unique blend of fantasy-reality! I also couldn't imagine working with better humans than the "1242 News Team" at MHS!

I have to acknowledge the roots of much of the music and writing with the concept of the Greys. "Fond old memories" for sure and we will "Sing thy song forever!"

Finally, I have dedicated this book to my three kids, as they are the ultimate blessing. Each of them continues to inspire me beyond words and spending time with them also teaches me what is truly most important in this life!

♮Sing a Song♮

Sing a song forget your sorrows
We're all going to make it here
Won't take long to remember
The only thing to fear is fear

Here I am again
Getting another test
That is what it comes to
I guess that is what's best

So many things can go wrong
Yet so many things are right
How I can get better
You know I'm here to fight

Sing a Song

Just want things to be simple
Want to live a happy life
Where people use the golden rule
And don't fill their hearts with strife

So many things I'm thankful for
So many things I've done
So many people, so much love
So much experience and fun

I just want to be better
I just want to be free
What can I do to solve this

Maybe it's not just about me

Everything is connected
Maybe the answer is just flow
Forget about your place in line
Focus more on the row

Sing a Song

We can get better
We can conquer this divide
We can help our sisters and brothers
Not worry about our sides

We all write our own life story
The superpowers are up to you
Who do you want to ride with?
How will you see it through?

Sing a Song

Let it flow
Find the space between
Let us all keep faith in love
Strong, confident, fluid and free

Pure is what we all can aim for
Forgive yourself
Forgive me
Forget about your bad situation
Forge a new direction and you will see.

Sing a Song
Maybe it's not just about me

Everything is connected
Maybe the answer is just flow
Forget about your place in line
Focus more on the row

Sing a Song

We can get better
We can conquer this divide
We can help our sisters and brothers
Not worry about our sides

We all write our own life story
The superpowers are up to you
Who do you want to ride with?
How will you see it through?

Sing a Song

Let it flow
Find the space between
Let us all keep faith in love
Strong, confident, fluid and free

Pure is what we all can aim for
Forgive yourself
Forgive me
Forget about your bad situation
Forge a new direction and you will see.

Sing a Song

㳄 Eyes Sea Mountain Water

Gazing at the mountain
Staring at the sea
Living life so freely
This is how we all should be

Now picture the idea
Of nature being vast
Of people living simply
And moving not so fast

Eyes Sea Mountain Water
Eyes Sea Mountain Water
Eyes Sea Mountain Water
Flowing on Me

Come along and share the feeling
It's not hard to realize
Just flow like the water
And open up your eyes

The positive vibrations
Will bring you to the Sun
Bake you with the energy
Of knowing you are one

Life's the real power
Everything is today
Practice with much laughter
Remember what you say

Right On 순

Right on this Earth I see
A better place for you and me
Right on this Earth I see
A better place for you and me

I'll take you to a place you've never been before
I want to show you the reasons that I'm fighting for
We could climb the mountains off the shore
We could dig down deep right into the core

Right on, right on yeah!

I want to know just how you feel about me
I want to let you climb on my cherry tree
We could be sly and avoid the fee
We could travel see anything you want to see

I want to live with you and have some fun
I want to have you and know that you're the one
We could be faithful and never have to run
We could grow together under this great big Sun.

Right On

About Time

I got the time if you got the time
You've got the time it's all about time
We've got the time it's all about time.

Now if you've got the time we can stop on a dime
Figure it out and make sure it rhymes
If you've got the time
It's all about time.

It's about time I get my feet moving
It's about time I get in the groove.
It's about time to stop the confusion
It's about time to handle our pollution

It's about time to focus on doing
Most of my life I've been misusing
Oh you know
It's all about time

Yeah the power in me and the power in you
If we take the steps we can see it through
It's about time
It's all about time.

It's about time we do our best
Working together that's the real test
It's about time
It's all about time!

So many people are just convinced
That fussing and fighting are part of the fix
It's about time

It's all about time

Time to stop the anger, time to stop the fights
Time for real leaders, who see the light.
It's about time
It's all about time

Not better than me, not better than you
Not far to the right or too far blue
It's about time
It's all about time

Now I've got the time if you've got the time
We can make time to stop on a dime
After all you know
It's all about time.

Time to slow it down enjoy the ride
Quit worrying so much just be by my side
We've got the time
It's all about time.

A wise man said, you can do what you choose
But you won't make it unless you give up the booze
After all you know
It's all about time.

Some see problems others see solutions
We are what we do enough mental confusion
It's about time
It's all about time!

Paradise in WVA

I was born with a silver spoon
Living away from it all
Conflict I did not know
Never faced that cannonball

Things were fine but it wouldn't last
I had to see this great big land
Headed north to start anew
My parents took me by the hand

Sometimes you can't see beauty
Until you view it from far away
Some things make you want to leave
Others make you want to stay

I'm talking about paradise in WVA

Living in a city they say you see more action
Everybody is searching for that satisfaction
Innocence here it passed right by me
Temptation was all that I could see

Sometimes I wish I could return
I know it seems funny with all that I have learned
Sometimes I get down on my knees and pray
I know we'll all be there someday

I'm talking about paradise in WVA

The Music's Trance

When the music plays in its crazy ways
I can't help but dance
Even when I'm low I seem to reach the high
Of the music's trance

Everybody's dancing
Everybody's singing with joy now
We all come together
Every girl and every boy

Everybody's reaching
Everybody's looking to the sky
We all can make it
Let the music make you fly

If you feel the trance then clap your hands
Everybody, everybody if you feel the trance
If you clap your hands you will feel the trance
Everybody, everybody if you clap your hands

That Sweet Old Feeling

Everyone was dancing and singing
When I came up to the house that day
Seemed like the Sun was looking right at me
Just then I knew what made me feel this way

Oh that sweet old feeling
That sweet old feeling when the guitars play
Oh that sweet old feeling
That sweet old feeling when the guitars play

Spirits were high and the bass was pumping
As we partied until the break of day
We all laughed and forgot our sorrows
The sky was black but there was a lot to say

Plant

Plant the seeds and watch them grow
Ride above and not below
Everything is in its row

Stumbled through the streets in silence
Right up to the river's bed
This old town it was in shambles
Thoughts were jumbled in my head

Plant the seeds and watch them grow
Ride above and not below
Everything is in its row

Just then a voice it whispered
From the sky it seemed to come
Though soft it was concise
It spoke to me just like a drum

Plant the seeds and watch them grow
Ride above and not below
Listen to the words that flow

Something Else to Do

Rolling home at the break of dawn
All night trip finally wearing off
I think I need something to see me through
There's always something else to do

They say that history returns
The fears rage and the wildfires burn
Picks me up when I'm feeling blue
There's always something else to do

We always talk about so much
Maybe that's our biggest crutch
Big plans that we never get to
There's always something else to do

Should we work on our playing?
Should we work with our tools?
Should we work on finding
Something else to do?

Something else to do, something else to do,
No matter how busy you are there's always
Something else to do

Something else to do, something else to do,
Oh oh something else to do

Children Unite ⇧

Children of the World we must unite
Children of the World we must unite
The ones in power may tell you to hate
What you need to realize is that's not our fate

Oh those poor misguided souls
They think they do right but they just don't know
They're drilling for oil because of greed
To fuel overconsumption that we do not need

All of our children can change their way
And we can build for a much better day

It's got to start with the children
We must teach them well
It's got to start with the children
We must all realize we drink from a common well

We cannot teach them to hate
They are not born to discriminate
That's not our way we need to plant the seed

Separation of Sight

Separation does not exist here
Just close your eyes and you'll see
It's the ultimate illusion
You need not have a key

So I walked along the river of separation
Skipping stones as far as the eye can see
I wrote these songs with a loving feeling
I hope you would agree

Take me down the road and to the farmland
Why don't you show me this land of the free?
We could fly over the cities of temptation
Oh how together we would be

The main thing that I've learned from all my travels
Is that all are one and one are all
This separation cannot remain here
We've got to watch that water fall

Close your eyes and you will see
You don't even need a key
You know we're all in this together
Sea to shining sea.

HE

He was a small town country boy
Was born on a farm
Separated from city life
It had its charm

Grew up shy, but always listened
Not quite one of the crowd
Politics and confusion
Lots of voices speaking loud

Moved to the city
Worked construction
And learned material ways
Got sucked in for quite a while
But finally learned to walk away

We can fight progress
Say no to new technology
But it seems no use
Watching monkeys on their cell phones
While others singing the blues

There's got to be a better way
We've got to get back to real communication
We're all zipped up with excess energy and just
don't know what to do

So Grey Today

So Grey today
    Some feelings just won't go away
        I know there is much love around
            Must be a method to just push play
        Feeling so down trying to figure out why
    Maybe it's time to just go get high
Feel like the energy is not flowing
    No clear end in sight
        Negative pull can be so strong
            And the energy can feel so right
        It's a funny thing
    How emotions and chemistry can mate
One minute you can conquer the world
    The next you just can't wait
        So many ways to escape
            Also to self-medicate
        You have tried everything
    You still come back and feel the same
Is there a test I can pass?
    Is there some secret to escape the shame?
        How can you sustain the highs?
            And limit the lows you feel?
        Make no mistake, the struggle is real.
    So many options out there
Funny how some people can make you dance
    If the ones around
        Don't build you up
            You won't have a chance
        Maybe there is a silver lining as they say
    Some people have never even felt this way
Does it give you perspective?

A lesson you can teach
    Is it a directive?
        So many people you can reach
    You can do this
Just remember to never give in
Temptations of giving up
    Thoughts of drowning creep right in
        One day, one thought,
            One moment at a time
    Try to see the light
Darkness can make you blind
So Grey today
    These feelings just won't go away
        I know there is much love around
            Trying to find a method
    To become unbound
Take me with you and help me with my pain
Understand my reality and help this love in vain
    Come closer this whole thing
        Can be cured with love
            Just hold me tightly
        Give me warmth, be my glove
    Always wanted to explore the limits
To take it up one notch
    Maybe this is the point
        Where you've had just too much scotch
            Finally learning to slow things down
    Brighten up your lens
Learning to live more simply
Loosen up these reigns
    Still grey, still today
        Maybe a touch of grey
            Is good anyway...

Magic J ✤

Let the magic happen
Let your feelings show
Let the energy inside you
Fill you up and let you grow

We all are here together
So let's enjoy the ride
So many differences among us
Just rolling on the rising tides

You can make your own choices
The ending is really up to you
We can see it from our own lenses
But that will only help a few

All the little children watching
Monkey see and monkey do
Feeling all stressed out and tired
Who's gonna see this through

Ooooh I see us racing
Up and down the streets
So many paths we can follow
Need to rest our weary feet

Can you give something back?
Can you just sit down and relax?
I know we're all good people
Do we have to relive the past?

It's all up to you

A Plan of Order ✢

There is an order
An order to our breed
We live in boxes
Surrounded by some trees

Go to the schoolhouse
So we can learn to see
What this nation
Wants us to believe

We sit in chairs
And take their tests
We want to perform
Better than the rest

If we do really well
We can rise to the top
Get the education
That makes us never stop

We seek to live a life
Surrounded by wealth
With no regard
For environmental health

Build cities by the dozens
Make products out of trees
Working even harder
For our own means

It's getting to the point

Where we don't even know
How to plant the seeds
And help them grow

Self-sufficiency
Does not seem to exist
And diversity
Gets lost in the mix

We alter our food
Our bodies and our genes
Will we soon not remember
What "natural" even means?

Cost of living is so high
We are draining our own fuel
Always wanting more
Bigger and better tools

Is this our nature?
Our chosen path?
Or could this just be
A political wrath?

We're often tempted
To leave well enough alone
But we must consider
That this world is our only home

Many fight for what is right
And don't worry about the plan
Looking for solutions
To help us change our hand

The power is in us all
And in this you can trust
The power is with the people
If they know they must

We can live together
We can find a way
Working hard for solutions
Building a better day

Endless Time ⑧

I really thought for just one moment you'd be mine
We would live together until the end of time
We would live together until the end of time
The end of time

That endless time
Just keeps on rolling back around
It really doesn't matter
Get your feet back on the ground
It really doesn't matter
Get your feet back on the ground
Back on the ground

Everyone is different
Yet we all are quite the same
Keep on writing keep on fighting
We'll set this town aflame
Keep on writing keep on fighting
We'll set this town aflame
This town aflame

Endless time yeah

No end and no beginning
We all just keep on spinning
No end and no beginning
It all just keeps on spinning

No end and no beginning
The race is on and no one's winning

So High and So Low

My highs are so high
But my lows keep getting lower

Open your eyes
Can't you see my disguise?

I know I'm all right
But I still feel like a fight
You want to sing along?
Just don't get it wrong

I know how to swim
But I just keep sinking
Want to open my eyes wide
But I just keep on blinking

It's hard to understand
I keep on sinning
It's a battle inside
I just want to be winning

Sometimes I feel like I'm king
Like I can conquer it all.
Then I feel like a pawn
And then I'm two feet tall.

I don't know who can understand
It's just how I feel.
Not sure who can help me
Who's ready to take the wheel?

I live from day to day
Trying to get better
Try to sing my songs
Looking for a love letter

Open your eyes
Can't you see my disguise?

My highs are so high
But my lows keep getting lower

Mindful ❖

The mind is a terrible thing to waste

So they say that the mind
Is a terrible thing to waste
If you focus hard
It will stay in place

So many of us
Don't really know
How to really use it
How to help it grow

We have infinite power
Of which to choose
It's a matter of deciding
When to light the fuse

If you live in the moment
And don't take it too fast
Your mind will help you
Your mind will last

There's positive and negative
Inside us all
Decide which you want
You make the call

Mindful decision to always be grateful
Mindful envision and disposition
This reality can help us all

Loss of Innocence

It all seems so innocent
It all seems so right

You thought you never should
You thought you never could
Just wanted to be cool
Not be anyone's fool

Started out with just a little
But you know it's the same old riddle
Knock, knock, who's there at your door?
You know who, they are always bringing more

One more drink one more hit
Oh I think your getting sick
You try to keep turning pages
But you're just slipping through the stages

Find yourself all alone
Taking hits just like a clone
Not a worry in your life
But moving slow and wasting time

Always fine unless it's gone
Until you're loved ones can't go on
Think you're in control
But in time it takes its toll

It all seemed so innocent
It all seemed so right

Started out so innocent
Never thought you would have to quit
So easy to slide right in
Battling with the self is a hard fight to win!

Face to Face

Ring, Ring, Text, Snap...
Put down your phone, I'm trying to reach you!

No skills? You can't fake them
A lot of drills, you can make them
If you really want the answers
Know yourself and mind your manners

Lots of people talking
Nobody is really listening
To the real day to day
And that's why this life is such a mission

Pass it on or pass it off
Angle of attack, no room for indecision
Understand it through religion
Or understand by intuition

Misunderstanding comes from interpretation
The same ideals but different pages

Try to move and watch nutrition
Try to limit screens of vision
It's as simple as addition
But we're still making bad decisions!

Teach Me ㊀

I'm a teacher
Not a preacher
Put down the cliffs notes
This is the full feature

What you gonna be?
How you gonna act?
Will you light it up?
Will you swing the bat?

You can ride the wave
Or the undertow
You can step right up
Or you can stay below

We're lighting sparks
And watching the glow
Gonna plant those seeds
And watch them grow

I'm a teacher
Not a preacher
Understanding is the goal
There is a procedure

Gonna help you out
Develop your powers
So you can bloom so big
Just like the flowers

Will you try your best?
Do you think you can?
Will you take the steps?
So you can be the best man?

I'm a teacher
Not a preacher
Step on the ice
I'm the crease creature

All I see is potential
Coming into my class
You can only limit yourself
But there's no free pass

I do think that
If you dig down deep
You just might find
What you sow is what you reap

Critical thought
Decision-making
Now you are ready
The world is for your taking

I'm a teacher
Not a preacher
Now it's up to you
You can reach her

I'm a teacher
Not a preacher
Ask yourself
Are you a believer?

Will you chase your dreams?
Will you train for hours?
Will you remember your roots?
Will you build a tower?

Ok I think you're ready
I have a bit of advice
Spread those wings
And keep your eye on the prize

Give more than you take
Treat others with love
Send it back to the children
Take the road up above

I'm a teacher
Not a preacher
Ask yourself
Are you a believer?

Can't Explain ⊕

Just can't explain how that beat makes me feel

The best science can't explain it
Inspiration is where it's at
Conversations with the Great Spirit
One love as he would say it

Don't fight the feeling
Just let yourself go
Make up your own mind
Ask yourself so

There's no hate in religion
There's no room for that
All is love and love is all
Use your glove not your bat!

Who wrote the book of love?
Who thought of destruction?
We all write our own book
Avoid the seduction!

If our children love one another
Then progress will be made
Lift others up
Step out of the shade!

Falling

I want you so bad
I think I'm falling for you
Give me all of your loving baby
And I'll give it right back to you

It's hard not to fall
My skies have been so blue
It's hard not to fall
For someone as amazing as you

Your skin so smooth
Those eyes and that smile
Every inch of your body
Constantly driving me wild

I think I'm okay
Just trying to take it slow
Just like riding our bikes together
Let's see where this path will go

Sights set high
Working out every day
Believing I can be somebody
That just won't give it away

Been playin' the field
With my eye on the ball
But with you it's a different feeling
Way too hard not to fall

Asking myself if I'm ready
Do I even know?
Is my life complete without you now?
Where will it all go?

I want you so bad
My skies are so blue
What I really want to say
Is that I've fallen in love with you

Find A Way

Ever since you left us
Things just haven't been the same
I don't know quite what happened
But I know that it is a shame

Sometimes I think
You got caught up in all the fame
Maybe there's a little bit
In all of us to blame

I used to think
That things were going to last
Now that very attitude
Seems like a thing of the past

I know you had your time
It must have been a blast
The only thing I wish
Is that it hadn't gone so fast

We must move on and find a way
To the break of dawn, we'll find a way
I know you'll be there when we find a way
Singing without care when we find a way

Thinking back now, I looked right through
If I remember right, I had a few
You taught me a love so kind and so true
I've never felt so happy, I've never felt so blue.

火 Tim 火

This is the fire
This is the burn
Are we going straight?
Are we taking a turn?

Life is rich
Don't waste it away
Kind hugs all day
That will make you stay

We named him Tim
He was our fire
And dancing with him
We got much higher

The woods are his fuel
We've got to feed him often
We've got to keep him stoked
Or his flames will be forgotten

His heart is like the one
Keeps us warm and keeps it fun
He always knows what to do
Sends the love to me and you

If you leave the circle
You will still see it from far away
You'll know that his light
Is ultimately here to stay

So warm and such fun
Have we even begun?
A ceremony of light
Energy of the Sun

Know

I call this know
I really gotta go
To the show
Cause all the people are gonna grow
When they hear the concerto
Jammin on the bongo, congo,
Banjo and the piano
So say bravo
Question the status quo
And try to overthrow
The ones who cannot show
Watch out for the undertow
Respect the overflow
Of the volcano and the tornado
Don't be a sideshow
Don't diss the low or the average Joe
Outgrow the so-so
For your power use hydro
And airflow
Be a virtuoso
Yo!

Attitude ★

Never give up
You just can't quit
Winners train more
Losers just don't get it

They say no limits
Only expectations
Want to take a flight?
Just make the reservations

You only hold yourself back
And that is the absolute truth
You can play on the field
Or you can watch from the booth

Your team has a dream
So keep it alive
Try to mess with the worker
And you'll get the whole hive

Attitude is everything
You can sing along
Attitude is everything
You can do no wrong

Fight until the end
Go through the wall
Keep your eye on the prize
And always stand tall

Welcome to the Mountains

❄ ❄ ❄ ❄ ❄ ❄ ❄ ❄ ❄ ❄ ❄ ❄

Welcome to the Mountains
Welcome to the top
All these snow covered Mountains
There is no need to stop

The snow bunnies are bundled
Still they look so hot
Get into the tub
And then we stir the pot

Money is flying in
That's never going to stop
Prices are so high
Everything still gets bought

Welcome to the Mountains
Welcome to the top
We've got snow-covered Mountains
But you still want to shop

Some people just amaze me
They can't even see
Paradise before you
All you do is freeze

Mountain surfing weather
So steep and deep
Riding on the powder
Keeping up the beat

Welcome to the Mountains
Welcome to the top
All these snow covered mountains
And you're still going to shop

If that's how it's going to be
I guess that's your plea
You take the green
I'll be in the trees

Break ✧

I've got to break away
I've got a takeaway
I will make them say all right

I've got to find a way
I've got to keep away
From the things that make me fight

I'm feeling strong
Nothing can go wrong
I'm finally getting through

Like a cannonball
Going through the wall
Fighting for the blue

So gather around
Just hear the sound
It's what we're meant to do

Keep the loving fun
Spark another one
It's up to me and you

Should we say I do?

✪ True Genius ✪

True Genius is a state of mind
True Genius is hard to find
True believers know who they are
True values go very far

True happiness
Cannot be bought or sold
True religions
Never get old

True belief in things
You cannot see
True being is
The best you can be

True Genius
What all can see
True Genius
Is more about "We"

True Feeling
Just letting go
True Performance
Is in the flow

True understanding
An attitude of win
True Genius
Is found within

Love Letter

I want to write it long
Don't want to get it wrong
Oh yeah
I want to write a Love Letter

Sometimes Love creeps up on you
Try hard but there's nothing you can do
Might as well just take a few
Write a Love Letter

Bring it back put down that screen
Think of your baby and the space between
Ink it down, fold and pass it to me
Write a Love Letter

Want to go back in time
Sing a simpler rhyme
Oh yeah
I want to write a Love Letter

This world can get you down
Crack you up and make you a clown
But there is a way to turn that upside down
Write a Love Letter

I want to write it long
Don't want to get it wrong
Oh yeah
I want to write a Love Letter

Diversity in Harmony

All creations were made so beautifully
No flaws, seriously

Now the natives of our land
We call them Indians
They didn't change their soil
See they were happy with what they had
They did not long for more

Diversity in harmony
Baby can't you hear them crying
Oh can't you hear the music?
Oh can't you feel the sound?

We're doing it all together
Just going round and round

Living here for generations
Being at peace with their needs
Satisfied with simple lives
They loved and did not greed

Taking only what you have to
One with nature is how you feed

Jamaica Jam ☼

There's an Island called Jamaica
Where they have a ball
No need for your soccer cleats
No need for the mall

Surrounded by nature's jungles
They learn how to let it grow
Teaching their children
Just to take it slow

Not be bound by material
Life in a simple way
The way it was intended
Saving just the day

Time to do a Jamaica jam
Bring us back the shore
Inspiration is the heart of all
It's the real common core

Time for a Jamaica Jam
All the kids dance and sing
Yes a real Jamaica Jam
We can let it ring

Tornado Dream ☳

What you need is a tornado
To lift you to the height
To see the world as beautiful
As it should have been left right

Why did we do this?
Why did we do that?
How did it get started?
How did we get so fat?

I've realized the problem
Is lurking deep inside
I've realized the problem
Is simply you and I

What you need is a tornado
To lift you to the height
To see the world as beautiful
As it should have been left right

We've got to change our lifestyles
We've got to start tonight
To cure our situation
To help us with the fight

Your life is a tornado
You listen to their lies
I hope that you'll discover
Before the day you die

What you need is a tornado
To lift you to the height
To see the world as beautiful
As it should have been left right

It came to me in a dream one night
And it carried me away
Oh I've seen the other side
And it sure looks beautiful

Some Lives We Remember

Some lives we remember
Some lives we don't
Does it only depend on
How much you rock the boat?

The energy is there
For us all to share
We better be witty
And we better care

The way that we use it
Is only up to us
We can decide to stumble
Or we can get on the bus

Once in a while
As I close my eyes
I pray to be better
And see through these lies

The lies of the big wigs
And ones in control
Who lead us into thinking
We're only in it for the gold

History books are written
Through a biased eye
What an artist wants to paint
Changing the color of your sky

Some lives we remember
Some lives we don't

∞ Happy Ending ∞

We all want a happy ending
We all want something to call our own
To be together with our loved ones
In a sea of shining stones

Trying to find the right solutions
Not to alter nature's course
Trying hard just to grow older
We may have to use a little force

Every story has a problem
To overcome before the end
Do we know if it's just waiting
Or in the hands of a good friend

Infinity's trial remains unanswered
We're all too busy with the task at hand
We all are one but seem divided
These are the questions we must ask our land

We all want a happy ending
We all want something to call our own
To be together with our loved ones
In a sea of shining stones

Happy ending, we'll all know it when it comes
Write yourself a happy ending today
It really does matter anyway

ABOUT THE AUTHOR

Jochen Hylbert was born in WV on a one hundred acre farm. He moved to Madison WI at age 9 where he grew up and attended high school.

Jochen holds a degree in Environmental Studies from Gustavus Adolphus College and a degree in Kinesiology & Exercise Science from the University of Wisconsin Madison.

Jochen has worked as a teacher, coach and advisor for the last 15 years in the Madison and surrounding area. Jochen is currently a health coach, trainer, consultant and owner of Advantagetrain.com.

Jochen is passionate about family, music, guitar playing, recreational athletics, gardening, spending time outdoors, mindfulness and maximizing human performance.

www.ingramcontent.com/pod-product-compliance
Lightning Source LLC
Chambersburg PA
CBHW051710040426
42446CB00008B/809